Pokemon

CW01501197

The Ultimate Pokemon Go Guide to Become the Very Best Trainer Out There.

Table of Contents

Introduction

Unless you were in deep cryogenic sleep or were abducted by aliens and just came back to civilization; you probably noticed that everyone around you is playing the new smartphone game: Pokémon GO! It's currently the most popular game out there and the hottest topic in social media and blogs. Every 90's kid either used to watch Pokémon the animated series back in the day or have at least once encountered this franchise. In those early days, collecting Pokémon trading cards and playing with them with your cousins, neighbors or friends were one of the best ways to have fun!

Pokémon abbreviated from the Japanese title 'pocket monsters' first came into this world via Nintendo. Pokémon was a video game for the original 'Game boy' and later, it was expanded for Nintendo 64 and many home console games. It was an instant hit and reached more than 200 million copies worldwide. Two years later in 1997, the animated series were developed by The Pokémon Company

International and the rest is history. A whole generation of kids in 90s and 2000s were brought up by this franchise. Pikachu and Ash were one of most favorite and popular characters in animated cartoon's history ever.

The adventures of Ash, Misty, and Brock with the humor of Team Rocket spanned in over 900 episodes of animated TV shows and 19 animated movies. Pokémon anime show is said to be one of the most successful TV franchise ever and one of the longest running animated TV shows out there. There are only two animated T shows in the world which are running longer than Pokémon, The Simpsons, and Arthur. It is more popular than SpongeBob

Squarepants! So it is not a wonder that when augmented reality game developer company Niantic partnered with The Pokémon Company and Nintendo and eventually came up with Pokémon GO!, it smashed all-time records of the most downloaded app ever in both iOS and Android defeating the previous record held by Candy Crush Saga.

What is Pokémon Go?

Pokémon Go is basically an Android and iOS based mobile game which uses augmented reality (a mixture of real life environment and clever integration of computer graphics) to give users interesting and unusual gaming experiences. Pokémon Go uses your phone's compatible GPS data and camera to show gaming elements such as Pokémon or Pokeshops in your device screen. Launched in 6th July initially in USA, New Zealand, and Australia, Pokémon Go allows its players to see, capture, battle, and train Pokémon in a virtual reality which is based on real places. By using your phone's camera and GPS, you can go to marked places in your surrounding area and capture Pokémon through your smartphone's screen. You basically roam around your neighborhood or even roam around the city (when you get addicted to it) to CATCH 'EM ALL with the app. It's a free app but you can use real money to buy PokeCoins and use those to buy features and virtual elements to be a better player and to catch more Pokémons. All you have to do is go out there and Catch'em All!

Why is it so BIG?

Everywhere in the social media, whether it is Facebook, twitter or a blog, you hear about Pokémon Go! You see pictures shared in your timeline of your friend catching some rare Pokémon in a very familiar place in your town. You see kids and grownups (90s kids) alike running around and catching Pokémon or battling with each other. All of these ought to make you wonder WHY it is suddenly so popular and everyone is into it?

There are many bloggers or game experts who have posed this question in the social media to gain some insight. And people have replied to them too. The most common reply to "Why is it so appealing?" is: "Dude! It's Pokémon!"

Yes, the very fact that it is Pokémon; the anime that has been a part of the childhood for so many 90's, 2000's kids and still a popular anime among the new generation, has played the greatest role for its growing fame. The nostalgia of the olden times has flourished again by this new app. Back in the day, kids imagined themselves as the likes of Ash, traveling the world and catching Pokémon, fighting with other Pokémon masters. Now that imagination has been somewhat coming to life by Pokémon Go. Now you can really CATCH 'EM ALL by simply installing an app on your smartphone. The app will give you real-life Pokémon adventure of your own and who doesn't want that? On top of it, the peer pressure that everyone is playing but you are not participating also made the difference. When you see your folks having fun and enjoying the game with their customized Pokémon, you will also feel the need to dive into the amazing word of Pokémon.

Another important fact is, Pokémon Go is very well designed augmented reality game. Going to real places and finding Pokémon allows the players to explore their own town or city which otherwise they might not have done before. Running around the city is a good cardio exercise and people always love the idea of combining fun with exercise. And you also get to meet new people and have new friends. After Pokémon Go has been released, you will be amazed to see how people's outdoor activity and social interaction have increased. Though it is mostly about Pokémon but still, it's a good thing. It has also paved the way for a new kind of father-son bonding. Parents are showing and teaching their kids what Pokémon is and how to catch them! In this case, parents know more than their kids about imaginary characters. Sometimes, parents are more enthusiastic in catching Pokémon than their kids. The sheer amount of people gathering in public places for the sake of catching Pokémon is staggering. Where there is a bunch of Pokémon, you see people coming from all directions, coming out of their homes and meeting, chatting with each other and having fun. This is the 21st century way of social interaction. This is the future of interactive gaming via augmented reality.

Pokémon Go 101 for dummies

Pokémon Go is taking over the world by storm! For past few weeks you might have dodged a few enthusiastic players who were walking down the streets with their eyes stuck in the smartphone. They were actually capturing Pokémon invisible to the naked eye. But the real question is, how do you play this super-popular game and how do you compete with other players?

The very core aspect of the game is to capture Pokémon. First, you make your own avatar within the game by customizing features like face, hair and eye color, dress, backpack and so on. When you finish making your avatar, you enter the vast wonderful Pokéworld! In the beginning, you start with one of this starter Pokémon options: Squirtle, Bulbasaur or Charmander. Each of them is unique in their own ways. But here is a Secret; you can actually walk away from these three and catch the most famous Pokémon of them all: Pikachu and start with it! See the Tips + Secret section to learn more about it.

Now, to capture your very first Pokémon, you just have to walk towards your chosen monster. The app will then automatically switch into augmented reality mode (it will turn on your front camera and you will see the Pokémon in front of you). When you see the Pokémon on the screen, you will also see a Pokéball at the bottom. Just swipe up and throw the Pokéball towards the monster to catch it. If it hits the Pokémon, the Pokéball will suck it inside and Wallah you have your first Pokémon!

If you want to catch more Pokémon, you have to go outside. Yes, to play this game you have to run around (literally!) the neighborhood to catch new Pokémon. You have to explore the map and find Pokémon in different places. This is the most interesting feature of Pokémon Go; it uses your GPS information to make a virtual Pokéworld matching the place you are currently living in. If you are in Miami it will create a virtual map of Miami in your app and you will have to explore real places to find new Pokémon.

When exploring the Pokéworld via Pokémon Go, you have to look out for three main symbols. The most important symbol is the 'shaking patch of grass' symbol. If you see this on your map, that means there is a Pokémon nearby. If you explore the place around that symbol, you are likely to find a new Pokémon hidden there. If you are ready and all excited, physically go near the shaking patch of grass to find and catch that Pokémon.

The next important symbol you should watch out for is the blue rotating icons. Those rotating cube icons represent Pokéstops. In Pokéstops, you get free eggs and Pokéballs to capture more Pokémon for your adventure. Pokéstops are commonly located in selected public places such as near famous monuments in your town, any historical markers or it could be near any popular art installation in your neighborhood. You have to physically walk near the Pokéstops and when you reach there, the icons will change into rotating photo disc of the place. If you swipe and spin that disc, it will generate free items in a bubble which you can collect. After you collect the items, the

Pokéstop icon will change its color to purple and you will not be able to get free stuff for a while until it refreshes itself (generally it's approximately five minutes). If you really want to collect a lot of Pokéballs and eggs then you have to hang around near the Pokéstops. In the beginning, Pokéstops will only produce three or four items at a time but when you eventually reach to level 5, you will get five to six items at once including new items such as Revives (which will grant you new life to your Pokémon) and Potions (for a quick heal for your Pokémon). These items are very useful when you are an experienced trainer and have access to PokéGym to battle with other players.

When you reach to level 5, you should look for the golden symbol which is the PokéGym. PokéGyms are less common on the map so you might have to walk long distances to find one. Gyms are usually in common public places and are often populated with players. You have to battle with other players Pokémon there to claim your superiority or simply to hold your turf. You can also claim a gym for yourself but for that, you have to leave one of your Pokémon there (it better be a powerful one!) to defend it from other players trying to claim it for themselves. PokéGym has colors (Red, blue or yellow) to show which team it belongs to. A PokéGym is usually claimed by a team of players and each member of the team can leave one of their Pokémon to defend it. If you want to take over a PokéGym, you have to assemble a team of your own (when you reach level 5, you have to choose one team).

Combat is another feature of Pokémon Go. In combat mode, you fight head to head with other player's Pokémon by tapping the screen to attack or swiping it to dodge and defend incoming attacks. You will need the new level 5 items (revive and potion) collected from Pokéstop after each battle. The revive will bring back your fainted Pokémon and potion will heal your injured Pokémon whenever needed.

You might wonder how to become a level 5 player. Here it is: there is no shortcut. You have to walk around and catch Pokémon to evolve them and soon you'll be a pro level 5 player. How? Each Pokémon has a number of candies and when you catch multiple of them, you can use them to evolve your Pokémon.

You can use real money to buy Pokémon Go's in-game money to purchase items like incubators (for the eggs). The eggs will hatch in the incubators and might give you rare Pokémon. But if you are really patient, you can earn in-game money by fighting with other players and leveling up.

These are the basics for Pokémon Go. Now all you have to do is get out there and have fun catching Pokémon!

Playing Pokémon Go on your smartphone

Before you get all excited to start your adventure with Pokémon Go, you should check if your phone is compatible with the app or not. If you do not have a powerful smartphone with good CPU and RAM, you might not be able to start your career as a Pokémon trainer. (oh bummer ☹).

But relax! You don't have to buy a $600 smartphone to play Pokémon Go. You just need a standard phone which has enough processing power to run the app and you will also need constant Wi-Fi and GPS.

For Apple devices, you must own iPhone 5 or above to play it and iOS 8 is a must. For android devices, the options are vast but keep in mind; you must upgrade the OS to at least

4.4 Kitkat. The marshmallow 6.0.1 will give you the best gaming experience. Preferred resolution is 720 x 1280 pixels for the best outcome (which is not optimized for tabs). A surprising fact is, Pokémon Go app does not work with any device which has Intel CPU in it. No one knows why.

You must consider buying a portable battery charger if you are planning to become a hardcore Pokémon Go player. Already there are feedbacks from the players that it drains a lot of battery. And be sure that you have an unlimited data plan or else all of your mobile data will vanish in a matter of minutes.

Source: Niantic Labs

PokéGym in a nutshell

Till now, there isn't any option to trade Pokémon with others or battle with other players directly. But you can battle with other players in PokéGyms. Gyms are visible on your map with a gray icon. It could also be colored (red, yellow, blue) icon with a Pokémon hovering on the top of it. If it's colored and a Pokémon is hovering that means that PokéGym is already claimed by a player and he or she is the gym leader. You have to defeat the gym leader (the player with the highest CP Pokémon becomes the gym leader) to claim that PokéGym for yourself. It is hard because a PokéGym is defended by a team of players and each of the players has one of their own Pokémon defending it. You have to battle for control over it!

Before starting the battle you have to choose six Pokémon to send to battle. You can use the basic types of attack like tackling or defend by swiping your screen or you can use the special attack on your opponent. Tapping the screen vigorously gives you fast attacks and it charges your special attack bar. If you can win the battle then eventually you can claim the PokéGym as your own and earn tons of items! There are few rules and regulations that you must know:

1. You cannot battle at a Gym unless you are a level 5 trainer.
2. You have to join a team (blue, red, yellow) to battle at Gyms.
3. Gain prestige to increase the level of the gym.
4. Add more Pokémon to the gym to defend and reinforce your turf.
5. Controlling the Gym is the key. Keep powerful high CP Pokémon there to guard it so that others can't defeat you and claim it.

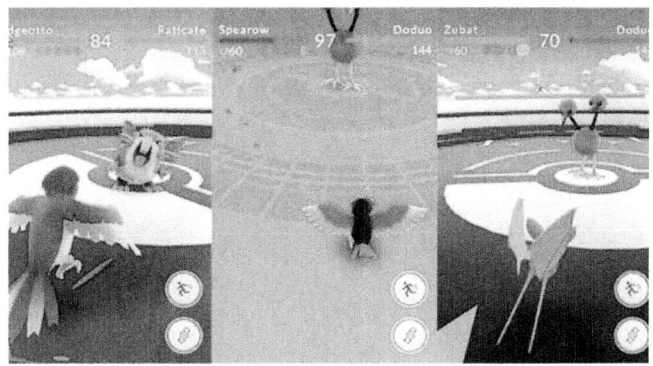

Those who are familiar with the original anime or have played the Pokémon games, they already know there are multiple types of Pokémon and each type have strengths and weaknesses to other types. This is very important because when you battle, knowing these types will give you the upper hand. If your opponent is battling with a water type Pokémon then you should use an electric type Pokémon to counter it. In this way, you can win a battle though your CP was lower than your opponent's Pokémon. Another fact a trainer must know is, same types of Pokémon can have different abilities. As an example, Oddish is a Grass/ Poison type Pokémon but two Oddishes can have different abilities- one having the grass attack move and one having the poison attack move. Each will be useful in different scenarios.

You should keep your roaster full of Pokémon with different abilities. Before boosting a Pokémon, see which ability is unique to your roster and focus on that. In this way, you can be a very effective trainer and can easily conquer the PokéGym.

Essential Tricks on Gaining XP

To gain the maximum output from your captured Pokémon, you must learn how to earn XP efficiently. The smart way is to learn the tricks and take advantage of the secret knowledge you have. Let's talk about how you are going to utilize your Pokémon and gain XP in the quickest way possible

Leveling up step by step gives you an advantage over many facets and you get access to new items to take advantage of it. Leveling up gives your Pokémon higher CP and you get better chance to win in a battle. In the basic levels, there are multiple activities which give you a certain amount of XP. These basic activities are:

1. Catching a Pokémon gives you 100 XP

2. Catching a new kind of Pokémon gives you 500 XP

3. Catching a Pokémon with curveball gives you extra 10 XP

4. For a nice throw of the Pokéball, you get 10 XP

5. For a great throw, you get 50 XP

6. For an excellent throw (when the green ring is the smallest), 100 XP

7. Evolving a Pokémon gives you another 500 XP

8. Hatching a Pokémon from the incubator gives you 200 XP

9. When you visit a Pokéstop, you get 50 XP each time.

There is also a way to double your XP via the 'Lucky Egg'. You don't get a lucky egg until you are level 9 but you can surely buy one with real money. Lucky eggs double your XP for half an hour. There are multiple ways you can use this special item. You can use it to level up many entry levels Pokémon or you can use it to evolve a Pokémon which requires only a few candies. The most efficient way to use it is to go near a Pokéstop and start evolving process there. If you still have a few minutes left of your half an hour, try luring more Pokémon to level them up. And if you are really super-confident that you can take out a PokéGym, you can use it to defeat the gym leader and claim a PokéGym for yourself.

Training and Leveling Up

As a Pokémon trainer, you have to level up continuously to gain access to new features and to be the best out there. It also affects how many times you encounter a rare Pokémon with high CP. So you have to learn how to level up the most efficient way to compete with other trainers in the rival gym.

The most efficient way is to gain XP (see the previous chapter). There are certain tasks and tricks which will give you easy access to XP. There are some special tricks too such us throwing a perfect Pokéball to catch a brand new Pokémon that will give you 700 XP.

Another great way to level up and gain XP is to visit the Gym (friendly or rival). You gain a good XP for battling your Pokémon in a friendly gym. Look out for easily beatable

Pokémon in the friendly gym and repeatedly train your Pokémon over and over.

You can maximize your XP by defeating a trainer in a rival gym. If you know your Pokémon very well and know the opponent's Pokémon roster, you can even beat them with a Pokémon that has a lower CP than your opponent's Pokémon. By using alternate types of Pokémon (as mentioned before; Grass for water types, water for fire types, fire for grass types and so on) you can smartly win a battle and gain XP to level up your trainer.

There is also a very effective way to level up fast by gaining XP in an easy way. You can catch many abundant Pokémon like Pidgey and evolve them to earn 500 XP each time. Pidgeys only need 12 candies to evolve so you can catch a lot of Pidgeys, transfer a few to earn candies to evolve the rest and get to level up very fast. Do not forget to activate Lucky Egg during this spree because each time you evolve a Pidgey, you get 1000XP when it's on. You can exploit the lucky egg to binge-evolve all of your available Pokémon if you plan ahead. If you still have some time, try to catch new Pokémon too. Till now there are 40 levels for a Pokémon Go trainer. Here is the list of how many XP you need to level up to the next one:

Level	XP Required to Reach Next Level
1	1,000
2	2,000
3	3,000
4	4,000
5	5,000
6	6,000
7	7,000
8	8,000
9	9,000
10	10,000
11	10,000
12	10,000
13	10,000
14	15,000

15	20,000
16	20,000
17	20,000
18	25,000
19	25,000
20	50,000
21	75,000
22	100,000
23	125,000
24	150,000
25	190,000
26	200,000
27	250,000
28	300,000
29	350,000
30	500,000
40	5,000,000 (Confirmed)

Pokestops: where to find them

Pokéstops are the places where you get free stuff like Pokéballs, revives, potions, eggs, and many other things. Basically, Pokéstops are marked in the Pokémon Go map with a rotating blue icon, as you already know. But what kind of real time places are Pokéstops?

Pokéstops are mostly landmarks or historically significant places or it could be a place of architectural or cultural significance. The landmarks may include murals, sculptures or even a well-known building in your area. You have to know where to look for a Pokéstop.

Naturally, it's obvious that big cities have more Pokéstops than rural areas as cities have more landmarks and well-known places. But even there the density of Pokéstops varies. The city center and the downtown areas have more Pokéstops than the suburbs. The recent Pokéstop data shows that, finding a Pokéstop could be a bit painful for those who live in a small town. Pokéstop data was created from Pokémon Go's creator, Niantic Lab's previous augmented reality game, Ingress. So the more densely populated the area is the more chances of finding Pokéstops. It will be a good idea to look for cultural districts or art districts to find many Pokéstops at one place.

Though it might look odd but Churches are said to be Pokéstops in many areas. Pokémon Go has chosen many churches to form the map to be a Pokéstop or even a PokéGym. If you don't have a museum or similar kind of cultural place, go for a church to find Pokéstop.

Big parks are most likely to have multiple Pokéstops. And it is a good thing, isn't it? You can jog while catching a Pokémon or just walk around the park while having fun with Pokémon Go. Gardens are also a suitable place to have Pokéstops. Since there are no cars in the parks or gardens, it is safe there to roam around rather than walking around in the streets.

There are reports from many players that they found Pokéstop inside a graveyard! Isn't it cool? You can now have a creepy-scary Pokémon adventure of your own. It will be more fun if go there at night with your buddies. It will be like Scooby doo gang uncovering secrets of Pokémon.

When you are not in class or during vacations, stroll around your college campus and you will definitely find a few Pokéstops there. College and university campuses have historic buildings, statues, and landmarks so it is bound to have a few Pokéstops of its own. If so then it will be a good thing for you if you are a student. You just have to visit the Pokéstop in between classes and get items whenever you need.

Museums and art galleries- these are the definite places where you will find Pokéstops. Take your buddies or family to visit any art gallery and you get two things at once: a tour of the gallery and free stuff from Pokéstop! Plan to visit the natural history museum this weekend and get some potions and pokeballs for FREE!

The bottom line is, any public place where people are likely to gather for social or cultural interaction, are bound to have a Pokéstop nearby. And if you are too lazy to find a Pokéstop for yourself, don't worry there are people who have made highly detailed maps of Pokéstops and places where you can get the most Pokémon or if you get lucky enough, find a rare Pokémon to catch!

Useful Pokemon Go Maps

Finding Pokéstops is a difficult task on its own and on top of that, finding places which are more likely to have a bunch of powerful Pokémon is harder to find. It is possible that you may have to walk all day but still could not find a single rare Pokémon, just bunch of Pidgeys and ratatas. To ease the struggle of the fellow players, brilliant tech-savvy people have come up with insightful maps which help players to identify places on the city maps where you are most likely to come across a powerful or rare Pokémon.

There are mainly three Pokémon Go maps which will give you an upper hand to find the Pokémon you are looking for. Learn to use these and you will be able to pinpoint some rarest of all Pokémon.

Pokecrew: Pokecrew is this killer app which can locate you on the map and track down exactly where are the Pokémon that is hiding in your neighborhood. Pokémon Go app does not show you distance instead it shows you footprints but this app will show you EXACTLY how far is the Pokémon from you. Rather than blindly roaming around to get what you need, you can now directly run for the Pokémon you want by installing this app. Though Pokecrew does not pinpoint the Pokémon like a laser guided missile but it gives you the closest estimate of where the desired Pokémon is and you have to literally hunt it down when you get there before someone else catches it.

Pokecrew uses user feedback to get more accurate information so day by day it is getting better and better. The maps are still going through development but the new updates via community-based feedback are making it an awesome Pokémon Go map. Just like the Pokémon , the pokecrew map is also evolving with latest data.

Gotta Catch'em All map: Till now this is the most comprehensive map of all. It tracks the location of nearby and distant Pokémon and classifies them into categories such as common type, uncommon type, rare type or ultra-rare Pokémon. The map is huge and you can see where the rarest Pokémon are in the city. If you have enough energy, pack your bags and head out for a long journey to catch some rare Pokémon. No matter how far it is, this map will update itself to track those Pokémon which has spawned within the city and will let you help prioritize your decision.

There is only one problem- this map is currently available only in Boston. So, if you are not living there, you can't use it...yet. The developers are working hard to expand it across the USA.

Pokemapper: Pokemapper is a community-based app. As long as there are people who are using it in your city, it will constantly keep updating itself and become better day by day. The more you use it, the more accurate information it will give you so start using it and encourage others to use it too. Though it is the least developed map, it has the highest potential as users grow.

These Pokémon Go maps/apps are for the dedicated trainers who are determined to become the best players. Using it could be tricky sometimes because the servers frequently get overloaded with incoming information and it takes time to refresh the map. But it is expected that these apps will get better as user demands are growing each passing   day.

Some Tips + Secrets

Footprints: When you tap the 'Nearby' window, you will see Pokémon with footprint icons just beneath it. Some will have one footprint and some will have more than one. These footprints roughly represent the number of meters or equivalent to that. One footprint means the Pokémon is approximately 20-100 meters away from you, two footprints mean they are roughly 100-300 meters away from you and three footprints mean it is equal or more than 300 meters from you. So technically the footprints represent distance and how far you have to walk to catch that Pokémon. So look out for evolved or high CP Pokémon though it might be further away from you. The more you walk, the more Pokécoins you get so don't hesitate to roam around as long as you like!

Transferring the weaklings: If you have multiple Pokémon of the same kind (let's say Pidgey), see which one has the lowest CP (combat points). There is no point on keeping a Pokémon which has very low CP if you have another one which has very good CP. In that case, keep the stronger one by tagging it with a star and transfer the weak ones to get a candy. You can then use that candy to evolve your other Pokémon (or power up). So, like this, get rid of all the extra weak Pokémon and get candies to evolve your stronger Pokémon.

Defender bonus: You can get free Pokécoins and stars if you have a Pokémon defending your PokéGym. You don't have to go to a Pokéstop to get new stuff. Get to PokéGym, claim it and leave a Pokémon there and you will get FREE Pokécoins (minimum 20 coins) every single day. You can use those to buy other items than eggs or Pokéballs (such as Lure Modules to attract Pokémon). So, get out there, claim a PokéGym and defend it with your strongest Pokémon!

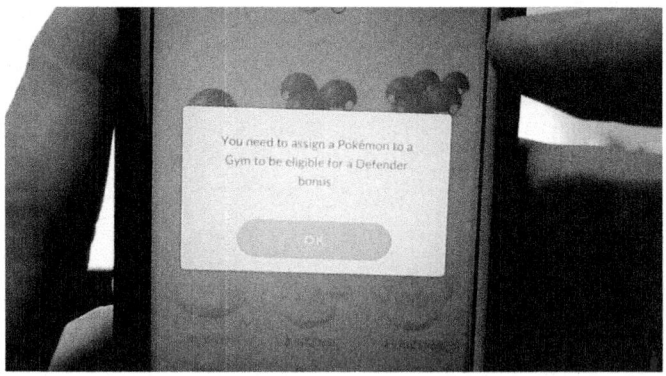

Use the ring to catch Pokémon: Catching Pokémon is not just about throwing the Pokéball at it. The more evolved Pokémon are harder to catch and sometimes they move around too. So throwing the Pokéballs at it aimlessly won't work. In this case, use the Ring reference. When you try to catch a Pokémon, you see a green ring within a white ring. The green ring gets smaller and smaller as you hold your Pokéball so; the most optimum way to throw a Pokéball is when the green ring is the smallest. If you throw it just when the ring is at its smallest size, you have the best chance to catch a Pokémon. If the ring is big, you might miss it and lose a Pokéball. Later you might see orange rings rather than green which means the Pokémon is harder to get and you might have to lure it (with barriers and other kinds of stuff) to calm it down and then when the ring turns green, you catch it.

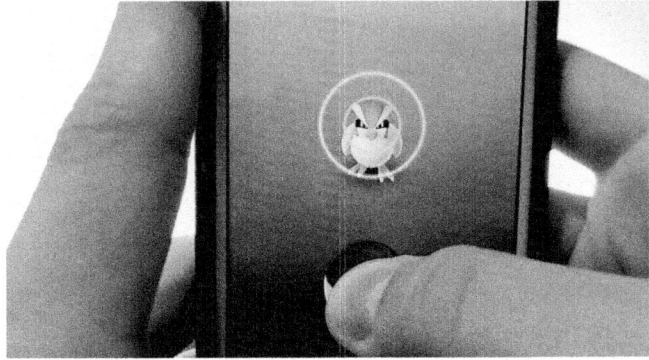

Curveball: While throwing the Pokéball, you can actually spin it to by moving your thumb round and round. That spinning Pokéball is called a curve ball and if you catch a Pokémon with a curve ball, you get an extra bonus! You will see glowing aura coming out of it when you spin it. But it's hard to catch a Pokémon with a curve ball, you have to master it. Use the green circle for the most effective result.

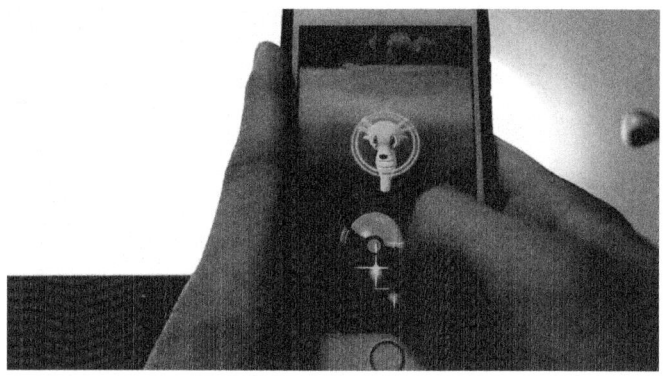

Use Incense to attract Pokémon: There is an item called 'Incense' which is like a perfume for your avatar that attracts different kinds of Pokémon. In the beginning, Pokémon Go provides you very limited amount of incense to use so use it very carefully. Pokémon lured by Incense can be seen only by you so only you can catch it; your friends won't be able to see them on their screen. You can buy incense from the shop with real money too.

Battery saver mode: If you exit from the app, you exit completely and your progress in the game is on halt. But if your battery saver or power saver mode is on (and your screen is black), everything will run in the background. Your eggs in the incubator will hatch, you will get notifications from Pokémon nearby and many other things. If you see your battery draining power too fast, try to exit the app completely. Or if you are concerned about your eggs, keep the battery saver mode on. :D

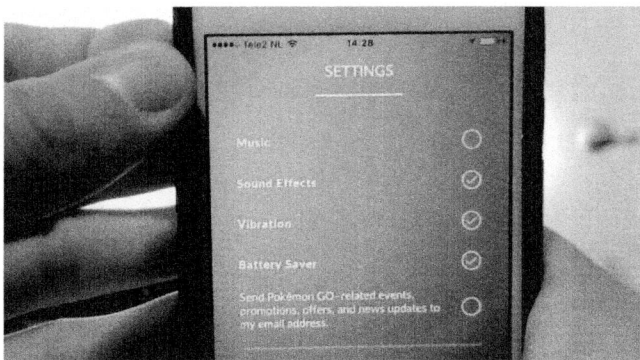

Don't waste healing potions: If you are trying to evolve a Pokémon which was used on gym battles and got injured in the process, don't

heal it with potions before evolving. Evolving Pokémon resets the health automatically so there is no need to heal it and waste a potion. Evolve the most powerful Pokémon with highest CP and get a fully fresh new Pokémon!

Lure Modules: Lure modules are items which attract all kinds of Pokémon towards it. You don't get a Lure Module until you get to level 8 but you can buy lure module from the shop with real money. A lure module will cost around $1 each and you can place it to a Pokéstop to attract Pokémon for half an hour. It is more fun and effective if you go to a Pokéstop with your team or friends and place a Lure Module there and since you all are on the same server, all of you will be able to see the incoming Pokémon and catch it. It is very effective if you go to a Pokéstop at night with your buddies and use it to catch as much Pokémon as you can. If you are in a densely populated public area (which is also a Pokéstop) and you place a Lure module, you will see people gathering near you to see and catch Pokémon. If there are enough Pokémon Go players around you then it is a good item to meet with other enthusiasts and fans of the game and chat with them.

Download offline Google maps for efficiency: Pokémon Go gets its map information from Google and if you download Google maps for offline use, your app doesn't have to update its map all the time. Go to Google maps setting and select the square grid (the most visited places around you) and download it. Pokémon Go will use this map to track your activity in the app. This way your battery also saves valuable charge.

Know the type of your Pokémon: There are many 'types' of Pokémon out there (grass, fire, water, electric etc). You must know which one is which type. Each Pokémon offsets each other during fights like the rock-paper-scissor method. Fire Pokémon are vulnerable to water, grass type Pokémon are vulnerable to fire and water is vulnerable to grass. Don't always go for higher CP Pokémon when you battle. The lower CP Pokémon can defeat a higher CP Pokémon if it's the exact opposite type.

Add variety to your Gym to defend well: Try to keep different type of Pokémon to the Gym you are defending. If there is already grass or fire type Pokémon from other teammates defending the PokéGym, try adding water type Pokémon then. This way when other players are battling with your Gym, they will face different types of Pokémon and it will be harder for them to claim the PokéGym.

Keep the Pokémon which has special moves: There are Pokémon who have special moves of their own other than tackling and body slam. If you have two Pokémon with the same CP keep the one which has a unique move and transfer the other one for candy. It's better to evolve the other one which will be more useful later on.

Getting stuff from Pokéstops: You already know you get free stuff from Pokéstop like Pokéball and eggs (if you're lucky), revives and other items. But here is the catch, unless you live or work near a Pokéstop, you cannot get that stuff often right? Here is what you can do; find a few Pokéstop in your neighborhood which are like ten minutes away from each other and visit them each. Each Pokéstop regenerates new items every five minutes so if you have multiple Pokéstop in a 5-10 minutes radius, you go to them in circles and get a lot of free items if you are that much willing to get those.

Catch Pokémon from home: When you are at home and doing nothing but do not feel like going outside, you can just sit on your couch or lie in your bed with your Pokémon Go app on. Turn off the music, keep the sound effect and vibration mode on, keep the battery saver mode on and turn on your Wi-Fi and just chill. Every now and then you will see notifications of new Pokémon popping up near you and you can just tap the Pokémon in the map to catch it. You don't have to go outside; you can easily catch one from your home via the map. This way you can catch as many Pokémon as you like and later, can transfer those for candies.

Catching a rare Pokémon: A rare Pokémon does not live in extreme places or you don't have to climb mountains to catch a rare Pokémon. Instead, your trainer level dictates which type of Pokémon you'll encounter. At the beginning, you will only see basic Pokémon like Zubats, Charmenders and the likes of it but later, when you level up to 10-11, you will see rare Pokémon with high CP in your map. But beware, powerful and rare Pokémon are harder to catch. They even break out of the Pokéball and run away. You may have to use luring items such as Rass Berries to catch them or later when you level up more, you may have to use Great Balls or Ultra Balls (which are more powerful than standard Pokéballs) to catch high CP rare Pokémon. Ultra Balls are hard to find and they hardly appear in Pokéstops. If you really are into it, buy some Ultra Balls from the shop.

Getting Pikachu as your first Pokémon: Very few people know that they can get Pikachu as you starter Pokémon. At the beginning, Pokémon Go forces you to choose a starter Pokémon from Squirtle, Bulbasaur or Charmander.

But you can simply walk away from them and just keep walking further. The map will refresh a couple of times and new Pokémon will spawn near you. Keep walking away from them until a Pikachu pops up in your map. When you see a Pikachu in your map, go near it and catch it with a Pokéball; now you've got Pikachu as your very first Pokémon!

The secret of evolving (evee)

Naming your Evee can change its evolution. The evolution of Evee (a very special Pokémon) differs according to its name. You can customize the name of your Pokémon from the edit option. This is a direct reference to the original Pokémon anime where there are three kinds of evolved Evees. They can evolve into Fire-type, water type or Electric-type Pokémon. If you name your Evee 'Sparky', it will evolve into Jolteon (an electric type Pokémon), if you name it 'Rainer' it will evolve into Vaporeon and finally, naming it 'Pyro' will allow it to evolve into Flareon. This is actually an Easter egg to the Pokémon anime where the evee brothers had three different types of eves. There could be more Easter eggs like this within the game. If you did not know this and already evolved your evee randomly then don't worry, next time assigns one of these names and get the definite evolution for your evee. Now you have to choose the name wisely and evolve smartly.

How to Hatch Eggs

During playing Pokémon Go, you might sometimes find Eggs in the Pokéstops with other free items. But, there are techniques of hatching eggs that you must know. Hatching eggs need a lot of work, it's not like battles or looking for Pokémon on the map. Different kinds of eggs hatch into different types of Pokémon. Pokémon Go gives you one free egg incubator at the beginning. Incubators are used to hatch eggs and it works this way: you have to walk a certain amount of distance (say 2km or 1.25 miles, 5km or 3.1 miles even 10km or 6.3 miles) to hatch them. In the meantime, your Pokémon Go app has to be on (keep the battery saver mode on and put your phone upside down so it will go in a standby mode but will keep track of your incubator). Don't try to be smart and drive 10km or take a bus to complete the 10km goal. The app measures distance by

GPS and your phone's pedometer. It can measure distance traveled per unit time i.e. it measures clock to see if you really walked there or not.

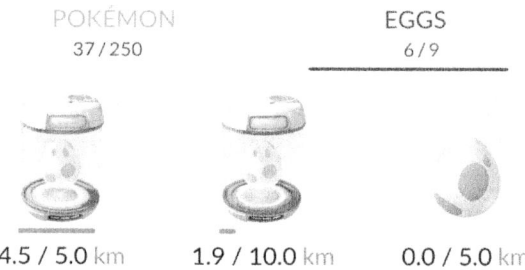

POKÉMON
37 / 250

EGGS
6 / 9

4.5 / 5.0 km   1.9 / 10.0 km   0.0 / 5.0 km

Using egg incubator could be tricky as you can use only a limited amount of time for limited eggs. Your starter incubator can hatch unlimited eggs for 2km. But you can buy other more advanced incubator from the shop. For 2km distance traveled, the eggs will hatch into basic Pokémon like Bulbasaur, Jigglypuff, Pikachu, Geodude, Weedle, Pidgey, Magicarp etc. But the underlying fact is, the more distance an egg needs to be traveled, the rarer the Pokémon it hatches. 5km eggs will give you pretty rare Pokémon such as Meowth, Abra, Horsea, Gastly, Vulpix, Vultrob and the likes.

But when you have to walk 10km, you can be sure that you will get rare Pokémon this time such as Onix, Evee, Jynx, Aerodactyl, Snorlax, Lapras, Hitmonlee, Electabuzz and much more like these. So whenever you decide to hatch eggs; keep all of these in mind and be cautious.

Things you should buy from the shop (with real money)

Every time you defend your gym, you get free Pokécoins to buy stuff from the shop. But if you really want to be ahead of other Pokémon Go players, you can use REAL money top buy useful items from the shop.

The best way to spend real money on Pokémon Go is to buy a pack of Pokécoins for $10. This will give you 1200 Pokécoins to spend and you can get a pretty good deal out of it. Don't just buy Pokéballs with this money because you get lots of those in Pokéstops. The best to spend them are like these: Buy a bundle of 8 incense with 500 Pokécoins which will give you up to four hours of Pokémon attraction. This is useful when you are just sitting in a park or stuck in traffic. Just use one of these and catch incoming Pokémon with ease. With the rest, buy three lucky eggs with 240 Pokécoins, two Lure Models worth 200 Pokécoins and a bag upgrade to add additional item slots which would cost another 200 Pokécoins. Lucky eggs give you double XP for half an hour (each) so you can make most out of your captured Pokémon and evolve them with a high XP. There are things you can do with lucky eggs activated which will boost your XP such as you can catch as much Pokémon as you can with the help of incense. You can evolve your Pokémon which usually gives 500XP but this time, you will get double! You can start hatching Pokémon which gives you 100XP per km traveled so using lucky eggs will increase your outcome. You can train or battle at Gym which will also give you extra XP. And if you really find a new Pokémon using curveball and throw a perfect catch, you will get at least 1000XP at once with the lucky eggs! Another useful item is the Lure Module and using it is a great way to make new friends! Lure modules attract Pokémon in a Pokestop for 30 minutes and everyone can see the incoming Pokémon. For a whole half an hour, a Pokéstop will be populated by hundreds of Pokémon when you place a lure module in it. You will see people coming out of their house or stopping their car to come and catch Pokémon near the lure module. You can have a fun Pokémon catching party with your friends by placing a Lure Module in the nearest Pokéstop (maybe outside of a café or in the park). This way you and your fellow peers get to have fun and you become the hero!

A Few FAQs

What are those paw prints?
Those are a rough estimation of distance. One paw prints= Pokémon in 100-meter radius, two paw prints = 300-meter radius and three paw prints = more than the 300-meter radius.

Why are there leaves rustling about in my map?
That leaf animation means there is a Pokémon nearby. If you go near, you can see a Pokémon in the map.

Does hatching eggs depend on speed or only distance?
During the egg hatching process, the app uses pedometer and GPS to track your speed. If you go faster than 12 mph, it will not count as distance covered. You have to WALK to cover the distance and cannot use public transport, cars or bikes.

What does that curve on the top mean when I select a Pokémon?
The arch above a selected Pokémon represents growth. You can use this as a reference to decide which Pokémon to evolve.

How can I trade Pokémon with my friends?
Right now, Pokémon Go does not have a trading feature. You can't even battle with your friends directly. Such kinds of social interactive features are yet to come.

I have too many duplicate Pokémon, what do I do with it?
Hand them over (transfer) to professor willow to earn candies. Use those candies to evolve other Pokémon.

What are the rewards of 'Leveling Up'?
Here is a chart of what you get when you Level up. Level 10 will earn you tons of things.

Level	XP Required	Total XP	Unlocked Items	Rewards
1	0	0		
2	1000	1000		Poke Ball x10
3	2000	3000		Poke Ball x15
4	3000	6000		Poke Ball x15
5	4000	10000	Gyms, Potions, Revives	Poke Ball x20, Potion x10, Revive x10, Incense
6	5000	15000		Poke Ball x15, Potion x10, Revive x5, Incubator
7	6000	21000		Poke Ball x15, Potion x10, Revive x5, Incense
8	7000	28000	Razz Berry	Poke Ball x15, Potion x10, Revive x5, Razz Berry x10, Lure Module
9	8000	36000		Poke Ball x15, Potion x10, Revive x5, Razz Berry x3, Lucky Egg
10	9000	45000	Super Potions	Poke Ball x20, Super Potion x20, Revive x10, Razz Berry x10, Incense, Lucky Egg, Egg Incubator, Lure Module
11	10000	55000		Poke Ball x15, Super Potion x10, Revive x3, Razz Berry x3
12	10000	65000	Great Balls	Great Ball x20, Super Potion x10, Revive x3, Razz Berry x3
13	10000	75000		Great Ball x10, Super Potion x10, Revive x3, Razz Berry x3
14	10000	85000		Great Ball x10, Super Potion x10, Revive x3, Razz Berry x3
15	15000	100000	Hyper Potions	Great Ball x15, Hyper Potion x20, Revive x10, Razz Berry x10, Incense, Lucky Egg, Egg Incubator, Lure Module
16	20000	120000		Great Ball x10, Hyper Potion x10, Revive x5, Razz Berry x5
17	20000	140000		Great Ball x10, Hyper Potion x10, Revive x5, Razz Berry x5
18	20000	160000		Great Ball x10, Hyper Potion x10, Revive x5, Razz Berry x5
19	25000	185000		Great Ball x15, Hyper Potion x10, Revive x5, Razz Berry x5
20	25000	210000	Ultra Balls	Ultra Ball x20, Hyper Potion x20, Revive x20, Razz Berry x20, Incense x2, Lucky Egg x2, Egg Incubator x2, Lure Module x2

How can I hatch eggs quicker?

There is no shortcut for hatching eggs. You cannot use transport to do it faster. The best way is to walk or jog along the park or get out there with your friends.

How do I become a Gym leader?

The trainer who has the highest CP Pokémon automatically becomes the gym leader. But if a PokéGym is already claimed and controlled, you have to defeat the Pokémon that is defending it to claim control over it.

What are the best Pokémon to evolve first?

In the beginning, Pidgey, Rattata, Weedle, Catterpie are the ones which use very few candies to evolve. And if you use the Lucky Egg (see how to hatch egg chapter) trick carefully, you can level up very fast with this Pokémon evolutions. Pidgeys are very common in public areas and evolving it will boost your XP as a beginner trainer.

Do weather, terrain and time of the day affect my Pokémon hunt?

Yes. Water based Pokémon is found near rivers and lakes, grass and rock types in the parks. Reportedly, ghost and dark type Pokémon are found during night. So, yes, in the real world, these actually affect what Pokémon you encounter.

How can I change my username or team name?

Currently, these options are not available. But you can edit and change the name of your Pokémon and in some cases; the evolution depends on it (see secrets of evolving chapter).

How many times does a Pokéstop refresh?
A Pokéstop refreshes once every five minutes. You can see the icon turning into blue from purple when it's refilled again with free items.

Some Weird and Fun Facts

Dead body

19-year-old Shayla Wiggins was looking for a water type Pokémon on July 8th near a river in Riverton, Wyoming. While exploring the area, she found a dead body floating in the water! She called 911 immediately but was disappointed because as she quit the app and dialed 911, she never found the Pokémon she was looking for.

Pokéstops and PokéGyms in weird places

Pokémon Go app is sending people to strange places to find Pokémon and placing Pokéstops and gyms in not-so-normal places like police station (in Australia), graveyards, churches, strip clubs even inside London's MI5 security headquarter! Some people are discovering that there are people gathering outside their house because it's a PokéGym! Some players are even trespassing into private property.

Pokémon Go is more popular than Tinder and as popular as Twitter

In less than a week, Pokémon Go was downloaded more than Tinder in android devices and almost catching up with Twitter! The average time spent by the user in Pokémon Go (43 minutes) is more than Instagram (25 minutes) or Snapchat (23 minutes).

It's FREE but Nintendo is earning money

Nintendo's share has gone up by 25% after the launch of Pokémon Go and it has earned more than $7 Billion on company value.

The most popular game ever

Pokémon Go is the most popular game ever beating candy crush saga. It has been downloaded by more than 21 million active users by July 12th.

Improvement in social life

By playing Pokémon Go, strangers are becoming friends and there are reports that say this game is actually beneficial for improving mental health as players are encouraged to go outside and experience the real world, and meet similar minded people in the process.

People leaving jobs and selling accounts on eBay

After the launch of the game, there are news that people are living jobs (in north London and in New Zealand) to play Pokémon Go. Some are selling high XP trainer accounts on eBay with a price as high as 7300 pounds!

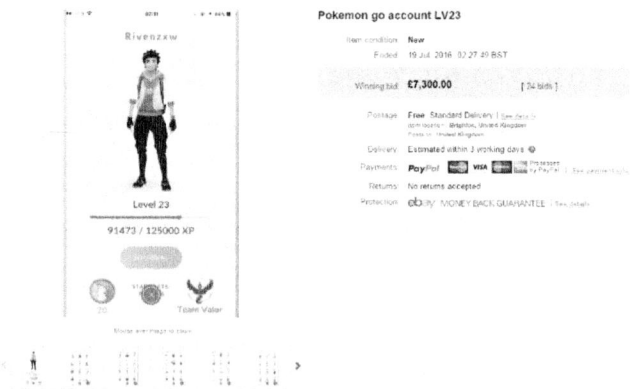

Beware of Fakes, Malwares, Glitches and Hackers

There are a few fake Pokémon Go apps out there. Keep away from them they can hack valuable information from your phone or attack with the virus. There were some apps recently like Pokémon Go Ultimate and Pokémongo which were reported and removed from Google app store. You can even face ads or featured apps like Pokémon Go cheats and codes but DO NOT install them or click them. Those apps contain harmful malware which can damage your phone's battery even the processor.

There are a few glitches which you might encounter during playing Pokémon Go. Your iPhone 6 might freeze time to time, in that case, disable your phone's LTE from **Settings>Cellular>Cellular Data** and turn LTE off.

Sometimes you will see that your avatar in the map is teleporting i.e. hopping across the map every few seconds. That means your GPS is not synced. In this case, you have to activate your full GPS because, in some android devices, GPS are usually off by default.

Sometimes, when you buy items with real money, it might now show in the inventory right away. Log out from Pokémon Go then log in again and it should be fixed. Some items may not be available in your country, in that case, check your Google wallet settings.

Always keep an eye on the updates and report bug fixes. And if randomly the app freezes try turning it off completely and on again (like the show IT crowd). Force stopping apps usually reset it to the last logged state.

What's Next?

In the recent San Diego Comic-Con, John Hanke the CEO of Niantic Labs who developed Pokémon Go gave a few insights on what's coming next. He said that the game will definitely evolve over time and it is only the beginning. Hanke even told the reporters that they have only included 10% of all the features they are planning to put in the game. Currently the most demanding and waited for feature, Pokémon Trading might soon be available for players. Pokéstops and Gyms will be for versatile and there will be special events during which, rare Pokémon will be available for capture for a limited period of time. There will be features that will allow forming a team of three with names from the original series and it will follow the same chain of command as the anime. In this way, clan forming and hierarchy system will be more interesting.

Conclusion

Surely, it is visible that Pokémon Go has set a
very high bar for future augmented reality
games. It is not only a fun game but the game
engine is fantastic and on top of that, it uses
the popularity of Pokémon and the very
nostalgia about the original show. Experts
predict that virtual reality and augmented
reality games are the next big thing and to
compete in the market, game developers has to
merge these two and come up with new ideas.
Wearable technologies like Google glass will
take to the next level. Wearable VR goggles will
make it more interesting to interact with the
game's characters and features in the near
future. Maybe then, you will be throwing
Pokeballs with your hands instead of the phone
screen. Pokémon Go will be a classic example
of augmented reality games in the future.
It will be very hard to beat Pokémon Go but
who knows, the future lies ahead. But for now,

all we can do is get the best fun out of this awesome game. So what are you waiting for? Go out there now, you GOTTA CATCH 'EM ALL!!

If You Want Free Best Selling Kindle Books Delivered Straight To Your Inbox

JOIN OUR FREE KINDLE BOOK CLUB!

BE PART OF THE CLUB

Thank you again for downloading this book!

If you enjoyed this book, then I'd like to ask you for a favor, would you be kind enough to leave a review for this book on Amazon? It'd be greatly appreciated!

Thank you and good luck! ☺

-Peter McDonald

Printed in Great Britain
by Amazon

57287831R00051